50 Low-Carb Dinner Ideas Recipes for Summer

By: Kelly Johnson

Table of Contents

- Grilled Lemon Herb Chicken
- Zucchini Noodles with Pesto
- Cauliflower Rice Stir-Fry
- Shrimp and Avocado Salad
- Grilled Salmon with Asparagus
- Chicken Caesar Salad
- Beef and Vegetable Skewers
- Spaghetti Squash Primavera
- Caprese Salad with Balsamic Glaze
- Stuffed Bell Peppers with Ground Turkey
- Grilled Portobello Mushrooms with Goat Cheese
- Eggplant Lasagna
- Grilled Shrimp Tacos with Lettuce Wraps
- Roasted Salmon with Garlic and Dill
- Cobb Salad with Chicken
- Keto BBQ Chicken with Cauliflower Mash
- Grilled Veggie Salad
- Zucchini Fritters with Sour Cream
- Cucumber Noodles with Tuna Salad
- Beef and Broccoli Stir-Fry
- Chicken and Avocado Lettuce Wraps
- Baked Cod with Lemon and Herbs
- Chilled Cucumber Soup
- Grilled Chicken with Creamy Garlic Sauce
- Spinach and Artichoke Stuffed Chicken
- Salmon Patties with Zucchini Ribbons
- Baked Eggplant with Parmesan
- Chicken Zucchini Casserole
- Grilled Steaks with Roasted Veggies
- Tuna Salad-Stuffed Avocados
- Baked Chicken Thighs with Roasted Brussels Sprouts
- Cauliflower Mac and Cheese
- Grilled Shrimp with Avocado Salsa
- Cabbage Stir-Fry with Pork
- Cauliflower Crust Pizza with Veggies

- Asian Cucumber and Shrimp Salad
- Roasted Chicken with Cauliflower Rice
- Pork Chops with Green Beans
- Spicy Keto Chicken Wings
- Grilled Veggie and Halloumi Skewers
- Chicken and Spinach Stuffed Mushrooms
- Garlic Butter Shrimp with Zoodles
- Tuna Steak with Avocado Salsa
- Grilled Steak with Chimichurri Sauce
- Eggplant and Mozzarella Roll-Ups
- Keto-Friendly Greek Salad
- Baked Lemon Herb Trout
- Cauliflower and Bacon Salad
- Zucchini Boats with Ground Beef
- Low-Carb Egg Salad with Lettuce Wraps

Grilled Lemon Herb Chicken

Ingredients:

- 4 boneless, skinless chicken breasts
- Juice and zest of 1 lemon
- 3 cloves garlic, minced
- 2 tbsp olive oil
- 1 tsp dried oregano
- Salt and pepper to taste
- Fresh parsley for garnish

Instructions:

1. In a bowl, mix lemon juice, zest, garlic, olive oil, oregano, salt, and pepper.
2. Marinate the chicken breasts in the mixture for at least 30 minutes, or up to 4 hours.
3. Preheat the grill to medium-high heat. Grill the chicken for 6-7 minutes on each side, until cooked through.
4. Garnish with fresh parsley and serve.

Zucchini Noodles with Pesto

Ingredients:

- 4 medium zucchinis, spiralized into noodles
- 1/2 cup pesto (store-bought or homemade)
- 1 tbsp olive oil
- Salt and pepper to taste
- Cherry tomatoes (optional)

Instructions:

1. Heat olive oil in a large pan over medium heat.
2. Add zucchini noodles and sauté for 2-3 minutes until slightly softened.
3. Toss the noodles with pesto sauce and cook for another 1-2 minutes.
4. Season with salt and pepper, and serve topped with cherry tomatoes if desired.

Cauliflower Rice Stir-Fry

Ingredients:

- 1 head of cauliflower, grated into rice-sized pieces
- 2 tbsp olive oil
- 2 eggs, beaten
- 1/2 cup diced carrots
- 1/2 cup frozen peas
- 1/4 cup soy sauce or tamari
- 2 green onions, sliced
- Salt and pepper to taste

Instructions:

1. Heat olive oil in a large skillet over medium heat. Add the grated cauliflower and cook for 5-7 minutes, stirring occasionally.
2. Push the cauliflower rice to one side of the pan and scramble the eggs on the other side.
3. Add carrots, peas, soy sauce, and green onions. Stir everything together and cook for another 2-3 minutes.
4. Season with salt and pepper and serve.

Shrimp and Avocado Salad

Ingredients:

- 1 lb cooked shrimp, peeled and deveined
- 2 ripe avocados, diced
- 1 cup cherry tomatoes, halved
- 1/4 cup red onion, thinly sliced
- 1 tbsp olive oil
- Juice of 1 lime
- 2 tbsp fresh cilantro, chopped
- Salt and pepper to taste

Instructions:

1. In a large bowl, combine the shrimp, avocado, tomatoes, and red onion.
2. Drizzle with olive oil and lime juice.
3. Toss gently to combine and season with salt, pepper, and cilantro.
4. Serve chilled.

Grilled Salmon with Asparagus

Ingredients:

- 4 salmon fillets
- 1 bunch asparagus, trimmed
- 2 tbsp olive oil
- Juice of 1 lemon
- 2 cloves garlic, minced
- Salt and pepper to taste

Instructions:

1. Preheat the grill to medium-high heat.
2. Brush the salmon and asparagus with olive oil and season with salt and pepper.
3. Grill the salmon for 4-5 minutes per side, or until cooked through.
4. Grill the asparagus for 2-3 minutes, turning occasionally until tender.
5. Drizzle the lemon juice over the salmon and asparagus before serving.

Chicken Caesar Salad

Ingredients:

- 2 grilled chicken breasts, sliced
- 4 cups Romaine lettuce, chopped
- 1/4 cup grated Parmesan cheese
- 1/4 cup croutons
- 1/4 cup Caesar dressing

Instructions:

1. Toss the chopped Romaine lettuce with Caesar dressing in a large bowl.
2. Add the sliced grilled chicken, Parmesan cheese, and croutons.
3. Toss again and serve immediately.

Beef and Vegetable Skewers

Ingredients:

- 1 lb beef sirloin, cut into cubes
- 1 red bell pepper, cut into chunks
- 1 zucchini, sliced
- 1 red onion, cut into chunks
- 1 tbsp olive oil
- 1 tsp garlic powder
- Salt and pepper to taste

Instructions:

1. Preheat the grill to medium-high heat.
2. Thread the beef and vegetables onto skewers.
3. Drizzle with olive oil and season with garlic powder, salt, and pepper.
4. Grill the skewers for 6-8 minutes, turning occasionally, until the beef is cooked to your liking.

Spaghetti Squash Primavera

Ingredients:

- 1 medium spaghetti squash
- 1 tbsp olive oil
- 1 cup cherry tomatoes, halved
- 1/2 cup bell peppers, sliced
- 1/2 cup zucchini, sliced
- 2 cloves garlic, minced
- 1/4 cup fresh basil, chopped
- Salt and pepper to taste

Instructions:

1. Preheat the oven to 400°F (200°C). Cut the spaghetti squash in half, remove seeds, and roast for 40-45 minutes until tender.
2. While the squash roasts, heat olive oil in a pan over medium heat. Sauté garlic and vegetables until tender, about 5-7 minutes.
3. Use a fork to scrape the spaghetti squash into strands and add it to the sautéed vegetables.
4. Toss to combine, season with salt, pepper, and fresh basil. Serve immediately.

Caprese Salad with Balsamic Glaze

Ingredients:

- 3 ripe tomatoes, sliced
- 1 ball fresh mozzarella cheese, sliced
- 1/4 cup fresh basil leaves
- 1 tbsp olive oil
- 2 tbsp balsamic glaze
- Salt and pepper to taste

Instructions:

1. Arrange the tomato and mozzarella slices on a serving platter, alternating them.
2. Tuck fresh basil leaves between the slices.
3. Drizzle with olive oil and balsamic glaze.
4. Season with salt and pepper and serve.

Stuffed Bell Peppers with Ground Turkey

Ingredients:

- 4 bell peppers, tops cut off and seeds removed
- 1 lb ground turkey
- 1 cup cooked quinoa or rice
- 1/2 onion, chopped
- 1 can diced tomatoes (14 oz)
- 1 tsp garlic powder
- 1 tsp dried oregano
- Salt and pepper to taste
- 1/2 cup shredded cheese (optional)

Instructions:

1. Preheat the oven to 375°F (190°C).
2. In a skillet, cook ground turkey and onion over medium heat until browned. Add garlic powder, oregano, salt, and pepper.
3. Stir in diced tomatoes and cooked quinoa or rice. Let it simmer for 5-7 minutes.
4. Stuff the bell peppers with the turkey mixture and place them in a baking dish.
5. Top with shredded cheese (if using) and bake for 25-30 minutes, until the peppers are tender.

Grilled Portobello Mushrooms with Goat Cheese

Ingredients:

- 4 large Portobello mushrooms
- 2 tbsp olive oil
- Salt and pepper to taste
- 4 oz goat cheese, crumbled
- Fresh basil leaves for garnish

Instructions:

1. Preheat the grill to medium heat.
2. Brush the mushroom caps with olive oil and season with salt and pepper.
3. Grill the mushrooms for 5-7 minutes per side until tender.
4. Top each mushroom with crumbled goat cheese and grill for an additional 2-3 minutes.
5. Garnish with fresh basil and serve.

Eggplant Lasagna

Ingredients:

- 2 medium eggplants, sliced into 1/4-inch rounds
- 1 lb ground beef or turkey
- 1 jar marinara sauce
- 1 cup ricotta cheese
- 1/2 cup shredded mozzarella cheese
- 1/4 cup grated Parmesan cheese
- 1 tsp dried oregano
- Salt and pepper to taste

Instructions:

1. Preheat the oven to 375°F (190°C).
2. Grill or bake the eggplant slices for 10-12 minutes until tender.
3. In a skillet, cook the ground meat over medium heat. Add marinara sauce, oregano, salt, and pepper, and simmer for 10 minutes.
4. In a baking dish, layer the eggplant slices, meat sauce, ricotta cheese, and mozzarella cheese. Repeat the layers.
5. Top with Parmesan cheese and bake for 25-30 minutes, until bubbly and golden.

Grilled Shrimp Tacos with Lettuce Wraps

Ingredients:

- 1 lb shrimp, peeled and deveined
- 1 tbsp olive oil
- 1 tsp paprika
- 1 tsp garlic powder
- 1 tsp lime zest
- Salt and pepper to taste
- Lettuce leaves (for wraps)
- 1/2 cup diced avocado
- 1/4 cup chopped cilantro
- Lime wedges for serving

Instructions:

1. Preheat the grill to medium-high heat.
2. Toss shrimp with olive oil, paprika, garlic powder, lime zest, salt, and pepper.
3. Grill shrimp for 2-3 minutes per side until pink and cooked through.
4. Assemble tacos by placing shrimp in lettuce wraps, and top with avocado, cilantro, and a squeeze of lime.

Roasted Salmon with Garlic and Dill

Ingredients:

- 4 salmon fillets
- 2 tbsp olive oil
- 2 cloves garlic, minced
- 1 tbsp fresh dill, chopped
- Juice of 1 lemon
- Salt and pepper to taste

Instructions:

1. Preheat the oven to 400°F (200°C).
2. Place salmon fillets on a baking sheet lined with parchment paper.
3. Drizzle with olive oil and sprinkle with minced garlic, dill, lemon juice, salt, and pepper.
4. Roast for 12-15 minutes, until the salmon is cooked through and flakes easily with a fork.

Cobb Salad with Chicken

Ingredients:

- 2 grilled chicken breasts, sliced
- 4 cups Romaine lettuce, chopped
- 1/2 cup cherry tomatoes, halved
- 1/4 cup red onion, thinly sliced
- 1/4 cup crumbled blue cheese
- 2 hard-boiled eggs, sliced
- 1/2 avocado, sliced
- 1/4 cup bacon bits
- 1/4 cup ranch dressing or your favorite dressing

Instructions:

1. Toss the Romaine lettuce with your choice of dressing.
2. Arrange the toppings (chicken, tomatoes, onion, cheese, eggs, avocado, and bacon) on top of the lettuce in separate sections.
3. Serve immediately, or toss gently before serving.

Keto BBQ Chicken with Cauliflower Mash

Ingredients:

- 4 chicken breasts
- 1/2 cup sugar-free BBQ sauce
- 1 head of cauliflower, chopped
- 2 tbsp butter
- 1/4 cup heavy cream
- Salt and pepper to taste

Instructions:

1. Preheat the grill to medium-high heat. Brush the chicken breasts with BBQ sauce and grill for 6-7 minutes per side.
2. Boil the cauliflower in a pot of water for 10-12 minutes, until tender. Drain and mash with butter and heavy cream until smooth. Season with salt and pepper.
3. Serve the grilled BBQ chicken with a side of cauliflower mash.

Grilled Veggie Salad

Ingredients:

- 1 zucchini, sliced
- 1 red bell pepper, cut into chunks
- 1 yellow bell pepper, cut into chunks
- 1 red onion, cut into chunks
- 1 tbsp olive oil
- Salt and pepper to taste
- 1/4 cup crumbled feta cheese (optional)

Instructions:

1. Preheat the grill to medium-high heat.
2. Toss the vegetables with olive oil, salt, and pepper.
3. Grill the vegetables for 4-5 minutes per side, until tender and slightly charred.
4. Top with feta cheese and serve warm.

Zucchini Fritters with Sour Cream

Ingredients:

- 2 medium zucchinis, grated
- 1/4 cup flour (or almond flour for keto)
- 1 egg, beaten
- 1/4 cup grated Parmesan cheese
- Salt and pepper to taste
- 2 tbsp olive oil
- Sour cream for serving

Instructions:

1. Squeeze the excess moisture out of the grated zucchini.
2. In a bowl, combine zucchini, flour, egg, Parmesan cheese, salt, and pepper.
3. Heat olive oil in a skillet over medium heat. Spoon the zucchini mixture into the skillet and flatten with a spatula.
4. Cook for 2-3 minutes per side until golden brown. Serve with a dollop of sour cream.

Cucumber Noodles with Tuna Salad

Ingredients:

- 2 large cucumbers, spiralized into noodles
- 1 can of tuna in olive oil, drained
- 1/4 cup diced red onion
- 1/4 cup chopped celery
- 1/4 cup mayonnaise
- 1 tbsp Dijon mustard
- Salt and pepper to taste
- Fresh dill for garnish (optional)

Instructions:

1. Spiralize the cucumbers into noodles and set aside.
2. In a bowl, combine the tuna, red onion, celery, mayonnaise, Dijon mustard, salt, and pepper.
3. Toss the cucumber noodles with the tuna salad mixture.
4. Garnish with fresh dill and serve chilled.

Beef and Broccoli Stir-Fry

Ingredients:

- 1 lb flank steak, thinly sliced
- 2 cups broccoli florets
- 2 tbsp soy sauce (or tamari for gluten-free)
- 1 tbsp oyster sauce
- 1 tbsp sesame oil
- 2 cloves garlic, minced
- 1-inch piece of ginger, grated
- 1 tbsp cornstarch
- 1/4 cup water

Instructions:

1. In a bowl, mix soy sauce, oyster sauce, sesame oil, garlic, ginger, and cornstarch with water. Set aside.
2. Heat a large pan over medium-high heat and sauté the beef slices for 3-4 minutes until browned. Remove and set aside.
3. In the same pan, stir-fry the broccoli for 2-3 minutes until tender.
4. Add the beef back to the pan and pour in the sauce mixture. Stir to combine and cook for an additional 2 minutes until the sauce thickens.
5. Serve hot with rice or cauliflower rice.

Chicken and Avocado Lettuce Wraps

Ingredients:

- 2 chicken breasts, cooked and shredded
- 1 avocado, diced
- 1/4 cup diced red onion
- 1 tbsp lime juice
- 1 tbsp cilantro, chopped
- Romaine lettuce leaves
- Salt and pepper to taste

Instructions:

1. In a bowl, combine shredded chicken, avocado, red onion, lime juice, cilantro, salt, and pepper.
2. Spoon the chicken mixture onto the center of each lettuce leaf.
3. Wrap the lettuce around the filling and serve as wraps.

Baked Cod with Lemon and Herbs

Ingredients:

- 4 cod fillets
- 2 tbsp olive oil
- 2 tbsp lemon juice
- 1 tsp dried thyme
- 1 tsp dried oregano
- Salt and pepper to taste
- Lemon wedges for serving

Instructions:

1. Preheat the oven to 375°F (190°C).
2. Place the cod fillets on a baking sheet lined with parchment paper.
3. Drizzle with olive oil and lemon juice, and sprinkle with thyme, oregano, salt, and pepper.
4. Bake for 12-15 minutes, until the fish flakes easily with a fork.
5. Serve with lemon wedges.

Chilled Cucumber Soup

Ingredients:

- 2 cucumbers, peeled and chopped
- 1 cup plain Greek yogurt
- 1/2 cup fresh dill
- 1/4 cup lemon juice
- 2 tbsp olive oil
- Salt and pepper to taste

Instructions:

1. In a blender, combine cucumbers, Greek yogurt, dill, lemon juice, olive oil, salt, and pepper.
2. Blend until smooth, then chill the soup in the refrigerator for at least 1 hour.
3. Serve cold, garnished with extra dill if desired.

Grilled Chicken with Creamy Garlic Sauce

Ingredients:

- 4 chicken breasts
- 2 tbsp olive oil
- 1 tsp garlic powder
- 1 tsp dried thyme
- Salt and pepper to taste
- 1/2 cup heavy cream
- 2 cloves garlic, minced
- 2 tbsp butter
- 1/4 cup grated Parmesan cheese

Instructions:

1. Preheat the grill to medium-high heat.
2. Rub chicken breasts with olive oil, garlic powder, thyme, salt, and pepper.
3. Grill chicken for 6-7 minutes per side, until fully cooked.
4. In a pan, melt butter over medium heat, then sauté garlic for 1 minute.
5. Add heavy cream and bring to a simmer. Stir in Parmesan cheese and cook for 2 minutes.
6. Pour the creamy garlic sauce over grilled chicken and serve.

Spinach and Artichoke Stuffed Chicken

Ingredients:

- 4 chicken breasts, boneless and skinless
- 1/2 cup spinach, chopped
- 1/2 cup artichoke hearts, chopped
- 1/4 cup cream cheese
- 1/4 cup Parmesan cheese, grated
- Salt and pepper to taste
- 1 tbsp olive oil

Instructions:

1. Preheat the oven to 375°F (190°C).
2. In a bowl, combine spinach, artichokes, cream cheese, Parmesan, salt, and pepper.
3. Cut a pocket into each chicken breast and stuff with the spinach and artichoke mixture.
4. Heat olive oil in a pan over medium-high heat. Sear the chicken for 3-4 minutes per side.
5. Transfer to the oven and bake for 20 minutes, until the chicken is cooked through.

Salmon Patties with Zucchini Ribbons

Ingredients:

- 2 cans salmon, drained and flaked
- 1/4 cup breadcrumbs (or almond flour for keto)
- 1 egg, beaten
- 2 tbsp Dijon mustard
- 1 tbsp fresh parsley, chopped
- 2 zucchinis, spiralized into ribbons
- Olive oil for frying
- Salt and pepper to taste

Instructions:

1. In a bowl, combine salmon, breadcrumbs, egg, mustard, parsley, salt, and pepper.
2. Form the mixture into patties and set aside.
3. Heat olive oil in a pan over medium heat and cook the patties for 4-5 minutes per side, until golden brown.
4. In another pan, sauté zucchini ribbons for 2-3 minutes until just tender.
5. Serve the salmon patties with zucchini ribbons on the side.

Baked Eggplant with Parmesan

Ingredients:

- 2 eggplants, sliced into 1/2-inch rounds
- 2 tbsp olive oil
- Salt and pepper to taste
- 1/2 cup marinara sauce
- 1/2 cup shredded mozzarella cheese
- 1/4 cup grated Parmesan cheese

Instructions:

1. Preheat the oven to 375°F (190°C).
2. Brush eggplant slices with olive oil and season with salt and pepper.
3. Place the slices on a baking sheet and bake for 15-20 minutes, flipping halfway through, until tender.
4. Top each slice with marinara sauce, mozzarella, and Parmesan cheese. Bake for an additional 5 minutes until the cheese is melted and bubbly.

Chicken Zucchini Casserole

Ingredients:

- 2 large zucchinis, sliced
- 2 cups cooked chicken, shredded
- 1 cup shredded mozzarella cheese
- 1/2 cup Parmesan cheese, grated
- 1/2 cup heavy cream
- 2 cloves garlic, minced
- 1 tsp dried oregano
- Salt and pepper to taste

Instructions:

1. Preheat the oven to 375°F (190°C).
2. Layer zucchini slices in a casserole dish.
3. In a bowl, mix shredded chicken, heavy cream, garlic, oregano, salt, and pepper.
4. Pour the chicken mixture over the zucchini. Top with mozzarella and Parmesan cheese.
5. Bake for 25-30 minutes until the cheese is bubbly and golden.

Grilled Steaks with Roasted Veggies

Ingredients:

- 2 ribeye steaks
- 2 tbsp olive oil
- Salt and pepper to taste
- 1 tsp garlic powder
- 1 tsp dried thyme
- 2 cups assorted vegetables (bell peppers, zucchini, onions)
- 1 tbsp balsamic vinegar

Instructions:

1. Preheat the grill to medium-high heat.
2. Rub steaks with olive oil, salt, pepper, garlic powder, and thyme.
3. Grill steaks for 4-5 minutes per side for medium-rare, or to desired doneness.
4. Toss vegetables with olive oil, balsamic vinegar, salt, and pepper. Roast in a 400°F (200°C) oven for 20-25 minutes.
5. Serve steaks with roasted veggies.

Tuna Salad-Stuffed Avocados

Ingredients:

- 2 ripe avocados, halved and pitted
- 1 can tuna, drained
- 1/4 cup mayonnaise
- 1 tbsp Dijon mustard
- 1 tbsp lemon juice
- 1 tbsp chopped parsley
- Salt and pepper to taste

Instructions:

1. In a bowl, mix tuna, mayonnaise, Dijon mustard, lemon juice, parsley, salt, and pepper.
2. Spoon the tuna salad into avocado halves.
3. Serve chilled or at room temperature.

Baked Chicken Thighs with Roasted Brussels Sprouts

Ingredients:

- 4 chicken thighs, bone-in and skin-on
- 1 lb Brussels sprouts, halved
- 2 tbsp olive oil
- 2 cloves garlic, minced
- 1 tsp paprika
- Salt and pepper to taste

Instructions:

1. Preheat the oven to 400°F (200°C).
2. Rub chicken thighs with olive oil, garlic, paprika, salt, and pepper.
3. Toss Brussels sprouts with olive oil, salt, and pepper.
4. Place chicken and Brussels sprouts on a baking sheet. Bake for 30-35 minutes until the chicken is cooked and sprouts are tender.

Cauliflower Mac and Cheese

Ingredients:

- 1 large head cauliflower, cut into florets
- 1 cup shredded cheddar cheese
- 1/2 cup heavy cream
- 2 tbsp cream cheese
- 1 tsp garlic powder
- Salt and pepper to taste

Instructions:

1. Preheat the oven to 375°F (190°C).
2. Steam cauliflower florets until tender.
3. In a saucepan, heat heavy cream, cream cheese, garlic powder, salt, and pepper until smooth. Stir in cheddar cheese.
4. Mix cauliflower with cheese sauce and transfer to a baking dish.
5. Bake for 15-20 minutes until bubbly.

Grilled Shrimp with Avocado Salsa

Ingredients:

- 1 lb shrimp, peeled and deveined
- 2 tbsp olive oil
- 1 tsp garlic powder
- Salt and pepper to taste
- 1 avocado, diced
- 1 tomato, diced
- 1 tbsp lime juice
- 1 tbsp chopped cilantro

Instructions:

1. Preheat the grill to medium-high heat.
2. Toss shrimp with olive oil, garlic powder, salt, and pepper. Grill for 2-3 minutes per side.
3. In a bowl, combine avocado, tomato, lime juice, cilantro, salt, and pepper.
4. Serve grilled shrimp with avocado salsa.

Cabbage Stir-Fry with Pork

Ingredients:

- 1 lb ground pork
- 4 cups shredded cabbage
- 1 tbsp soy sauce (or tamari for gluten-free)
- 1 tbsp sesame oil
- 2 cloves garlic, minced
- 1-inch piece of ginger, grated
- Salt and pepper to taste

Instructions:

1. In a pan, heat sesame oil and cook garlic and ginger for 1 minute.
2. Add ground pork and cook until browned.
3. Stir in cabbage and soy sauce. Cook for 5-7 minutes until cabbage is tender.
4. Season with salt and pepper, then serve.

Cauliflower Crust Pizza with Veggies

Ingredients:

- 1 head cauliflower, riced
- 1/4 cup Parmesan cheese, grated
- 1 egg, beaten
- 1 tsp Italian seasoning
- Salt and pepper to taste
- 1/2 cup pizza sauce
- 1 cup assorted veggies (bell peppers, mushrooms, onions)
- 1/2 cup shredded mozzarella cheese

Instructions:

1. Preheat the oven to 425°F (220°C).
2. Microwave riced cauliflower for 5 minutes, then squeeze out excess water.
3. Mix cauliflower with Parmesan, egg, Italian seasoning, salt, and pepper. Form into a crust on a baking sheet.
4. Bake for 10-12 minutes until golden.
5. Spread pizza sauce, top with veggies and mozzarella, and bake for another 10 minutes.

Asian Cucumber and Shrimp Salad

Ingredients:

- 1 lb shrimp, cooked and peeled
- 2 cucumbers, thinly sliced
- 1 tbsp rice vinegar
- 1 tbsp soy sauce (or tamari for gluten-free)
- 1 tsp sesame oil
- 1 tsp honey
- 1 tbsp sesame seeds
- 1 tbsp chopped green onions

Instructions:

1. In a bowl, mix rice vinegar, soy sauce, sesame oil, honey, sesame seeds, and green onions.
2. Toss cucumbers and shrimp with the dressing.
3. Chill for 15 minutes before serving.

Roasted Chicken with Cauliflower Rice

Ingredients:

- 4 chicken thighs, bone-in and skin-on
- 1 large head cauliflower, riced
- 2 tbsp olive oil
- 1 tsp paprika
- 1 tsp garlic powder
- Salt and pepper to taste

Instructions:

1. Preheat the oven to 400°F (200°C).
2. Rub chicken thighs with olive oil, paprika, garlic powder, salt, and pepper.
3. Roast chicken on a baking sheet for 30-35 minutes.
4. Sauté cauliflower rice in a pan with olive oil for 5-7 minutes until tender.
5. Serve chicken with cauliflower rice.

Pork Chops with Green Beans

Ingredients:

- 4 pork chops
- 1 lb green beans, trimmed
- 2 tbsp olive oil
- 1 tsp garlic powder
- 1 tsp dried thyme
- Salt and pepper to taste

Instructions:

1. Preheat the oven to 375°F (190°C).
2. Season pork chops with olive oil, garlic powder, thyme, salt, and pepper.
3. Sear pork chops in a pan for 2-3 minutes per side, then transfer to the oven for 15-20 minutes until cooked through.
4. Sauté green beans in a pan with olive oil for 5-7 minutes.
5. Serve pork chops with green beans.

Spicy Keto Chicken Wings

Ingredients:

- 2 lbs chicken wings
- 2 tbsp olive oil
- 1 tsp paprika
- 1 tsp cayenne pepper
- 1/2 tsp garlic powder
- Salt and pepper to taste
- 1/4 cup hot sauce
- 2 tbsp butter, melted

Instructions:

1. Preheat the oven to 400°F (200°C).
2. Toss chicken wings with olive oil, paprika, cayenne pepper, garlic powder, salt, and pepper.
3. Place wings on a baking sheet and bake for 40-45 minutes, turning halfway through.
4. In a bowl, mix hot sauce and melted butter. Toss cooked wings in the sauce and serve.

Grilled Veggie and Halloumi Skewers

Ingredients:

- 1 block halloumi cheese, cubed
- 1 red bell pepper, cubed
- 1 zucchini, sliced
- 1 red onion, cubed
- 2 tbsp olive oil
- 1 tsp dried oregano
- Salt and pepper to taste

Instructions:

1. Preheat the grill to medium heat.
2. Thread halloumi, bell pepper, zucchini, and onion onto skewers.
3. Brush with olive oil and sprinkle with oregano, salt, and pepper.
4. Grill for 8-10 minutes, turning occasionally until veggies are tender and halloumi is golden.

Chicken and Spinach Stuffed Mushrooms

Ingredients:

- 12 large mushrooms, stems removed
- 1 cup cooked chicken, shredded
- 1 cup spinach, chopped
- 1/2 cup cream cheese
- 1/4 cup Parmesan cheese, grated
- 1 clove garlic, minced
- Salt and pepper to taste

Instructions:

1. Preheat the oven to 375°F (190°C).
2. In a bowl, mix chicken, spinach, cream cheese, Parmesan cheese, garlic, salt, and pepper.
3. Stuff the mixture into mushroom caps.
4. Place on a baking sheet and bake for 20-25 minutes until mushrooms are tender and filling is golden.

Garlic Butter Shrimp with Zoodles

Ingredients:

- 1 lb shrimp, peeled and deveined
- 2 zucchini, spiralized into zoodles
- 2 tbsp butter
- 2 cloves garlic, minced
- 1/4 tsp red pepper flakes (optional)
- Salt and pepper to taste
- 1 tbsp lemon juice
- 1 tbsp chopped parsley

Instructions:

1. In a pan, melt butter and sauté garlic and red pepper flakes for 1 minute.
2. Add shrimp, cook for 2-3 minutes per side until pink.
3. Toss in zoodles, lemon juice, salt, and pepper. Cook for 2-3 minutes until zoodles are tender.
4. Garnish with parsley and serve.

Tuna Steak with Avocado Salsa

Ingredients:

- 2 tuna steaks
- 2 tbsp olive oil
- Salt and pepper to taste
- 1 avocado, diced
- 1 tomato, diced
- 1 tbsp lime juice
- 1 tbsp chopped cilantro

Instructions:

1. Heat a grill or pan over medium-high heat.
2. Rub tuna steaks with olive oil, salt, and pepper. Sear for 2-3 minutes per side for medium-rare.
3. In a bowl, mix avocado, tomato, lime juice, cilantro, salt, and pepper.
4. Serve tuna steaks topped with avocado salsa.

Grilled Steak with Chimichurri Sauce

Ingredients:

- 2 steaks (ribeye or sirloin)
- Salt and pepper to taste
- 2 tbsp olive oil
- 1 cup fresh parsley, chopped
- 1/4 cup fresh cilantro, chopped
- 2 cloves garlic, minced
- 2 tbsp red wine vinegar
- 1/4 cup olive oil
- 1/4 tsp red pepper flakes (optional)

Instructions:

1. Preheat the grill to medium-high heat.
2. Season steaks with salt, pepper, and olive oil. Grill for 4-5 minutes per side for medium-rare, or to desired doneness.
3. In a bowl, mix parsley, cilantro, garlic, red wine vinegar, olive oil, red pepper flakes, salt, and pepper.
4. Serve steaks topped with chimichurri sauce.

Eggplant and Mozzarella Roll-Ups

Ingredients:

- 2 large eggplants, thinly sliced lengthwise
- 1 cup marinara sauce
- 1 cup shredded mozzarella cheese
- 1/4 cup Parmesan cheese, grated
- 2 tbsp olive oil
- 1 tsp Italian seasoning
- Salt and pepper to taste

Instructions:

1. Preheat the oven to 375°F (190°C).
2. Brush eggplant slices with olive oil, sprinkle with Italian seasoning, salt, and pepper. Roast for 15-20 minutes until tender.
3. Spread a spoonful of marinara sauce on each slice, top with mozzarella, and roll up.
4. Place roll-ups in a baking dish, top with remaining marinara sauce, mozzarella, and Parmesan cheese.
5. Bake for 20-25 minutes until bubbly and golden.

Keto-Friendly Greek Salad

Ingredients:

- 2 cups romaine lettuce, chopped
- 1 cup cucumber, diced
- 1 cup cherry tomatoes, halved
- 1/2 cup Kalamata olives
- 1/4 cup red onion, thinly sliced
- 1/2 cup feta cheese, crumbled
- 2 tbsp olive oil
- 1 tbsp red wine vinegar
- 1 tsp dried oregano
- Salt and pepper to taste

Instructions:

1. In a large bowl, combine lettuce, cucumber, cherry tomatoes, olives, red onion, and feta cheese.
2. In a small bowl, whisk together olive oil, red wine vinegar, oregano, salt, and pepper.
3. Drizzle the dressing over the salad, toss to coat, and serve.

Baked Lemon Herb Trout

Ingredients:

- 2 trout fillets
- 2 tbsp olive oil
- 2 cloves garlic, minced
- 1 lemon, sliced
- 1 tsp dried thyme
- Salt and pepper to taste
- Fresh parsley for garnish

Instructions:

1. Preheat the oven to 375°F (190°C).
2. Place trout fillets on a baking sheet lined with parchment paper.
3. Drizzle olive oil over the fillets and sprinkle with garlic, thyme, salt, and pepper.
4. Lay lemon slices on top of the trout.
5. Bake for 15-20 minutes or until the fish flakes easily with a fork.
6. Garnish with fresh parsley before serving.

Cauliflower and Bacon Salad

Ingredients:

- 1 head cauliflower, chopped into small florets
- 6 slices bacon, cooked and crumbled
- 1/4 cup green onions, chopped
- 1/2 cup mayonnaise
- 1/4 cup sour cream
- 1 tsp Dijon mustard
- Salt and pepper to taste

Instructions:

1. Steam or blanch cauliflower florets until tender but still crisp. Let cool.
2. In a large bowl, combine cauliflower, bacon, and green onions.
3. In a separate bowl, mix mayonnaise, sour cream, Dijon mustard, salt, and pepper.
4. Pour the dressing over the cauliflower mixture and toss to coat.
5. Refrigerate for at least 30 minutes before serving.

Zucchini Boats with Ground Beef

Ingredients:

- 4 medium zucchinis, halved lengthwise
- 1 lb ground beef
- 1/2 cup onion, chopped
- 1 cup marinara sauce (sugar-free)
- 1 cup mozzarella cheese, shredded
- 1 tsp Italian seasoning
- Salt and pepper to taste

Instructions:

1. Preheat the oven to 375°F (190°C).
2. Scoop out the center of each zucchini half to create a boat. Set aside.
3. In a skillet, cook ground beef and onion over medium heat until beef is browned. Drain excess fat.
4. Add marinara sauce, Italian seasoning, salt, and pepper to the skillet. Simmer for 5 minutes.
5. Fill each zucchini boat with the beef mixture. Top with mozzarella cheese.
6. Place zucchini boats on a baking sheet and bake for 20-25 minutes or until zucchini is tender and cheese is melted and bubbly.

Low-Carb Egg Salad with Lettuce Wraps

Ingredients:

- 6 hard-boiled eggs, chopped
- 1/4 cup mayonnaise
- 1 tbsp Dijon mustard
- 1/4 cup celery, finely chopped
- 1/4 cup green onions, chopped
- Salt and pepper to taste
- Lettuce leaves for wrapping

Instructions:

1. In a bowl, mix chopped eggs, mayonnaise, Dijon mustard, celery, green onions, salt, and pepper.
2. Spoon the egg salad onto lettuce leaves and wrap them up.
3. Serve immediately or refrigerate until ready to eat.

www.ingramcontent.com/pod-product-compliance
Lightning Source LLC
LaVergne TN
LVHW061955070526
838199LV00060B/4139